D1500901

Interior Joy Inc.

ISBN 978-0-557-00254-2

Order online at:

http:www/InteriorJoy.com

http:stores.lulu.com

Space Photography compliments of

http://hubblesite.org

The
New
Human

DeAnne Hampton

One Love
One World

DeAnne

It is a very fierce Soul that wants to have life and deepen the well always of our understanding and awareness of Self - through other. It is through grace and a luminous mind that one can appreciate the exquisite way spirit invites us into our own participation with the rich complexities of this life. We all must truly see clearly now, allow the LOVE in fully and get about the work of authenticating SELF into the power and service of a magnificent transformation of this rare blue planet. The New Human is an invitation of pure essence, love and promise for ALL people... it is impregnated with an unapologetic yet unassuming sweeping up of all who are ready to love Self and BE the truth of who they are.

Come.... let your voice be heard.

—DeAnne Hampton

TABLE OF CONTENTS

Unraveling The Mystery ~
Steps on the Path of Becoming

The New Day

So many stories come to us from an intentional weaving of past and future. If they are non-fiction or autobiographical in nature, they will often begin with the experiential history of the author, an accounting of sorts where she has been or what he brings to the table in knowledge and credibility. Or, if fiction, the story will offer some enticing intrigue as to the nature of the plot and the alluring potential of a duplicitous outcome.

I am choosing to do neither because it is indeed, a new day for humankind. A day and time where a new part of the brain is being activated on our planet and as a species, we have the capacity to attune to and act upon a higher form of intelligence than we have in the course of our history. The details of my experiential reality are not nearly as important as the intuitive ability you consciously engage with which to interact with this information. I am bringing to you this knowledge through a level of commitment and devotion that defies even my own intellectual understanding. And it is that very same devotion and commitment to the One Life, the One Love, the One Truth from which we all came, in you, that has aligned you with this insight and illumination in your now. There is after all only One. And that One that is you, that is me, that is every other entity engaging reality at this time from the capacity and understanding of their own being, represents a super consciousness and deeper mind that is, at long last, asserting itself into the conscious thoughts and perceptual awareness of all of humankind. The unknown is making itself known. It is subtle and not so subtle, patient yet unrelenting, a quiet revolution within, awakening to the destined evolution of a species that has re-membered its true origin.

If you have been sensing the vibrational impulses in your reality, if you have found your thought forms in deep contemplation, questioning what you are observing, yet not quite sure of how to chart a new course in your own reality, much less the greater reality of a seemingly lost world, take heart. You are a descendent of a hierarchy that quite literally is deeming to interact with you, right in this moment, through a genetic structure and cellular imprint that is present in the stars. Be fearless in coming out of your slumber. Illusion cannot tread where truth walks, deception cannot dwell where light shines and humanity can only evolve as each individual dares to bring intelligent awareness to wherever the shadow resides.

The following reflection and discourse is the intelligent and fearless awareness of the divine mind expressing through one being. It matters not who the individual entity is. What matters is that we choose to listen and to take action in living the light of our cosmic mastery as stewards of the New Earth.

The Evolution of a Master

Every great Master evolved through the fire of experience.

The inspiration for the title of this book came from observing life. So much spiritual thought and current discussion, under-standably so, is about the increase in vibrational influence upon the planet at this time. There is no question that the reality we find ourselves in throughout the world is very much a state of crises for humanity. Our state of health . . . economically, physically, environmentally and spiritually, is in such a distorted divide between our heart center and ego attachments, that it would seem only a great upheaval could shift the balance from mind to heart.

The new human is in truth, a new consciousness. Within the Soul of Humanity is the intent to participate in a conscious transformation that will expand awareness beyond the limitations of time and space into the multidimensionality of the Universe. This new consciousness is not something that can or even will happen by a decision that we make. We have become much too imprisoned by our illusions to make that leap. The new human is an evolution of beingness that takes place when one determines 1st, to acknowledge that they really have no control over the reality they have built around themselves and then to allow their heart to guide them into the unknown future of their Soul's intent.

It is no longer acceptable or even possible to live so deeply cocooned in the comfort of a known existence, practicing spirituality from the sideline of a well-ordered

3D life. This too, is an aspect of ego asserting itself into the frame of reference that the mind has judged as acceptable and even noble. Every Soul on the planet in this momentous now chose a beautiful gift in the opportunity to evolve a new world, transforming humanity by achieving mastery in a way that is totally new. We have been preparing for this lifetime through many generations and we all bring the potential of transmutation and completion not only for the whole of our ancestral lineage, but for the experience of 3rd dimensional expression.

Yet we must reclaim our power and our willingness to be loved. We are learning to ascend through an experience of duality that is so very foreign and harsh to our inherent light. This full-scale revolution can either be by default, resulting in devastation and loss of life for the identity we have so come to define ourselves by in today's world. Or it can be transformed into an evolution of consciousness that embodies the vibrational momentum to lift the collective frequency of planet Earth into a new paradigm: a new light frequency that carries all the wisdom, all the love and all the power we will ever need. In remembering that the process of transformation is a co-operation between the light and each individual, the higher light and frequency of our own potential will assist us to bring about change.

And what exactly is that new paradigm? Well, the simplest way to answer the question that truly only your expansiveness can, is to start with the summit of your own reach.

Humanity is currently vibrating at the top edge of fourth dimensional frequency. The third dimensional energy of the personality construct and the fourth dimensional energy of the emotional aspect, are folding up into fifth dimensional principle and essence. Indeed, human consciousness is spiraling to a higher harmonic supported by the torsion waves of the higher realms, all to initiate and enhance a global shift in consciousness. The veils that have protected mankind from the onslaught of previous incarnations of experience are being lifted. In this process, we will be increasingly able to attune to different dimensions in the same way as the turn of a radio dial allows you to tune into different channels. You will know when you are vibrating with fourth dimensional frequencies when you have a conscious awareness and experience of communication with the animal kingdom and elemental beings from the devic kingdom.

There are Masters walking amongst us in this reality today, as well as an entire population of the Inner Earth that vibrate and live the way of fifth dimensional principle exclusively; compassion, unconditional love, harmony, joy and effortless manifestation. They use their creationary powers to call forth everything that they need instantaneously from a center of heart consciousness. This is a frequency where there is no fear, no judgment, no entitlement and no separation. It is the essence of being within every Soul currently living on Earth and, in fact, many light workers here today came from the fifth dimensional plane of existence prior to incarnating into this reality.

So, how do we get from where we are in this now, a consciousness of exclusivity, conditional love, extreme separation and an obsessive attachment to form, to a new consciousness where balance and harmony are the foundation of the wisdom we embody and live?

The first and most defining answer to that question is," who do you know yourself to be, truly?" Are you living in the light of that truth with all of your being and wisdom or are you clinging to the attachments of form and an identity you have come to accept as your known?

I have no agenda in what I have to share with you, no desire to change your mind or convince you of something that is not your truth. It is an immense Love that motivates and inspires the decisions and actions I engage.

What I know in my heart's intelligence is that the Earth is not to be destroyed and it is my choice to be one of the many working toward that end. My chosen life experiences have prepared me well to assist in the conscious expansion of humanity at this time. Ultimately, every person has to find the voice of God within and listen to only that. You must surrender to the still small voice over every other person and thing to bring your choices and actions into alignment with the destiny of your future self.

I have come to shine light for the One purpose of bringing about a shift in consciousness, a turn in the prism of your current understanding. Clearly, the whole of humanity cannot jump the chasm of frequency between third dimensional reality and fifth dimensional living all at once. But there are those of us who agreed to be the energetic forerunners of this planetary expansion, knowing that each person that awakens to a new light of understanding and beingness, empowers the momentum of the Collective.

Energy cannot move without the magnetic attraction of new frequency grids. As those who have refined their focus and freed their attachment energy enough to step out fully into the new energies begin to do so, they are doing so on behalf of all of human kind. Of which, each is destined eventually, to evolve to.

The new human must necessarily be fearless. The new human must become adept at engaging the divine mind versus the thought form of the egoic mind in making choices and decisions for the collective and unity consciousness over the dictates and control of the mental plane. We must necessarily move away from the energetic trenches of the individual "I" that is so concerned with the needs of self that there is no longer a distinction between consciousness and form. As a race, we have become what we own, know and can gather around us for the safety and protection of an illusory sense of self. It is time for the illusion and separation to cease. The deception in our own lives of who we are and how we live has bore an entire reality of existence that is very much governed by deception in many forms, levels and guises. Deception dwells wherever Truth is not wholly present.

We live in a time of unfolding prophecy and the new Earth is upon us. She will manifest by force and devastation or by the light of a great sun that is opening to us energetically at this time. The light is there to penetrate the shadow and lift the veils that for so long we have allowed to become our truth. This current portal in evolution on planet Earth is to allow for a radical transformation of human consciousness. The Great Mother is giving birth to this new consciousness and new life for all those that trust the formless over form and re-member that the essence of their authentic nature and purest frequency is calling them back home. Destiny beckons.

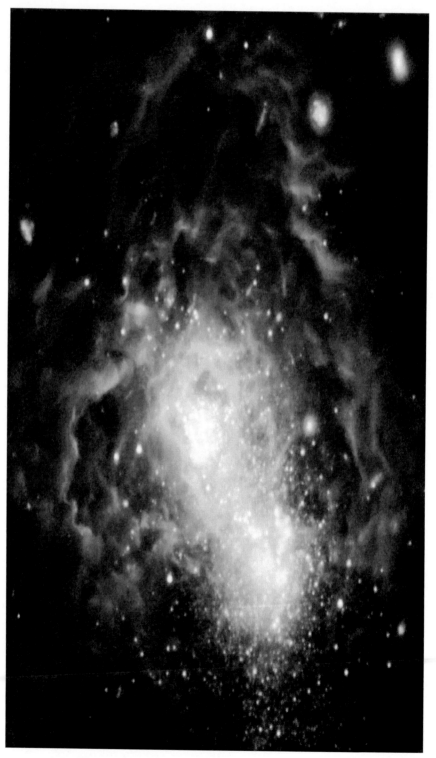

Looking At The Illusion

"People are like stained-glass windows. They sparkle and shine
when the sun is out, but when the darkness sets in, their true
beauty is revealed only if there is light from within."
Elizabeth Barrett Browning

One inevitable result of the planetary evolution is that we must be more accountable to our own process. This shift is really happening, and quickly! We have gotten somewhat complacent in our internal stretch, in part, because there have been so many predictions and markers for potential events for so long.

Since the Harmonic Convergence of 1987, lightworkers and spiritual teachers have been preparing for change to various extents. Yet, human nature leans easily in the direction of the path of least resistance when it comes to familiarity and comfort zones. Change is not a strong suit for the personality aspects of our being, especially when you've long been dressed for a party that seems to be some unpredictable future event. The unpredictable will continue to be a constant, but the rumblings and evidence of unsettling events economically and environmentally, as well as the ensuing threats to the very life and freedom of the known reality, will continue to accelerate at alarming rates.

The crises upon us at this time can no longer be stalled or held together by the false sense of power and control we have all succumbed to in varying degrees over the course of our history. We must either allow these new energies to support the need to let go of what we cling to in fear of losing our attachments, or we'll be swept into the density and shadow of those forces that are bound by illusion and separation.

It hurts to grow. Anyone that tries to tell you differently is not being completely honest. We must hold our focus and trust on that which is limitless and eternal with the promise of rebirth, over the fear of the unknown. When you truly begin to let go, to unwind the insane rhetoric of the egoic mind, you begin to sense and feel and assimilate these loving and powerful energies that are here on our behalf. There is an excitement building energetically that, as you continue to extend your reach, carries the momentum of your creative power to fully engage and become adept at living in the unknown. There is magic in the mystery, yet we cling tenaciously to the survival of our egoic self.

I have had countless lightworkers say to me, " I am not willing to lose my house, be alone, not live in comfort, give up this or let go of that." That is the ego talking and in control of your reality. First of all, those statements all revolve around loss, limitation and ultimately fear of death. Secondly, they reflect attachment energy, which keeps you in the sleep of social consciousness and imprisoned by the matrix. You are in effect saying that having these things is worth not belonging to your Self: that you trust the mechanisms of this reality more than you trust the Creator of the Multiverse.

The Source of all creation wants for us infinitely more than we could dare imagine for ourselves. But if we insist on filling our lives with transient form over what is timeless and true, we are willingly creating lives of pain and meaningless pursuits that will never be satisfied.

This is a time for ACTION. The task we have before us is huge, stunning in nature and easily excused to making the responsibility for change someone else's. No longer can we compartmentalize what we view as the greatest problem we face on the planet at this time. All the traditional structures and value systems have become so manipulated by the false power and desires of the ego, nothing but a new age and shift in consciousness will turn the page to a new history.

There is, indeed, a Collective Human Consciousness, a group energy that consists of the energy dynamics of every person that has ever lived on this planet over the entire course of its history. Every thought, feeling, emotion, word spoken and action taken has and continues to go into this composite energy of the Collective Human Consciousness. That is both the good news and the less than encouraging, as well. One need not look too far into the events of our history to see evidence of why in today's world, we are governed by so much deception and greed and senseless killing of our brothers and sisters, so that we have the most toys when the day is done. These energies of acceleration moving through us right now are for change. They are forcing us to look at what we have suppressed, denied and ignored and at the same time, providing the frequencies of potential to rise above what has so paralyzed us in fear. The habits, attitudes and behaviors of our Collective Consciousness grew out of the very same energies we have been unwilling to look at in ourselves. That is where the action must necessarily take place today and that is what will create the repository for the new consciousness of the future Earth.

There have been many Ascended Masters and evolved beings that have walked the Earth over thousands of years.

Their presence was not just to teach us the principles of a more authentic and evolved way of living in the world. Each one of them opened the portal of Christ Consciousness and the potential for us to realize it within ourselves. Their mastery and power, their wisdom and their love is a vibration very much present and available to us in the Collective of Human Consciousness, as well.

Each day that we live our light, that we love as they loved, practice compassion, understanding and forgiveness as they did and walk with peace within our being, we are creating the new consciousness one act of awareness at a time.

Truly, we are living in a profound period of activation. We are poised on the precipice of a world that will become the new Eden. We must cease the inauthentic expression of who we are as individuals and be willing to look at the illusions we have allowed to manipulate our daily lives. They are holding us back personally and globally. We are radiant beings of light that came to this planet in this now to be shining representatives of the new age. It is time to get serious about owning our attachments to this plane. Be impeccably honest with yourself over the way you justify anger, selfishness, resentment, jealousy, gluttony, greed or even discontent. "It's not that bad, " is no longer an acceptable way of deflecting energy from those illusions at which you fear looking.

Christ Consciousness is here. It is all around you energetically, for you to continually draw upon in raising the consciousness you currently vibrate. There is so much love (the most powerful frequency of the cosmos) here right now, extending a new Presence of power to you and on your behalf. Stop settling for the half lived version of your life and begin today to clean the shadows and cobwebs from your own closet. They may be hidden from everyone other person on the planet and for countless years, but they are not hidden from the unrealized potential within you, waiting to be set free. The future of the world depends on you. And when the 6 billion sovereign beings on this planet truly understand that, we will all rise together as One, to a brand new day.

Thought Forms As Powerful Creators

"The way we live our lives echoes through eternity."

The Gladiator

When first reading the title of this chapter, I am sure many of you had the immediate response, "oh, I already know that concept. I am very conscious and aware of my thought process." But are you? There comes a time on every seeker's journey, a nexus point of understanding, when he or she must decide whether or not to cross the great divide between the vibration and beingness of two worlds. So profound in implication and significant to spiritual mastery is this reach that a soul will often spend many chosen lifetimes building vibrational momentum, before being ultimately prepared for this leap. And leap is an apt metaphor for what constitutes a cellular, multidimensional transformation of the entire being.

No longer will you think, take in experience or even be able to live in the arena of your known reality in the same way. This is the place where the Soul's truth is revealed and great warriors emerge into the light of day. It is the point every master and great teacher, every disciple of the light, must eventually step consciously up to, befriend, exchange frequency with and eventually conquer. It is not for the fearful, the faint of heart or slaves of thought. It is, in fact, the only way to freedom from thought and an impenetrable, supreme awareness of Self. When it is your time, chosen in the light of all eternity, to cross fearlessly between the two worlds of form and formlessness, you will know - and you will follow that knowing until your last breath.

Your thoughts, physiology and myriad of emotions in this moment, having just taken in the above information, will reveal much about where you are in your evolution and what may well be on the very near horizon for you. Most especially so because of the time we are in as a species. What is so magnificent about this NOW is that we are being vibrationally encoded, attuned and rewired in our individual expansion process by the planet's own expansion process. Ready or not! This is truly unprecedented and exciting from the awareness of our spirituality. As the deeper mind of our being knows that all life and levels of consciousness are intrinsically one with the life of the living organism that is our planet, we once again can look to the Earth in support of our own forward movement.

Whether it is a conscious remembrance or not, we are ultimately here to align our personality aspect with our Soul essence, healing the duality of a world governed by separatism. The way in - to the new Earth and to the promise of a peaceful and sustainable future, lies in the transcendence of thought; the ability to engage your experience while rising above thought and thus connecting with the timeless, formless awareness of your infinite nature. Each time you can be in an experience as an observer, seeing the judgments, the unconscious impulse, to separate and define and categorize and classify within the constructs of your known identity, you are acting as a sovereign being. Unfortunately, it is easier and more prevalent to become slaves, not only to our own reactionary perceptions, but to be unconsciously manipulated by the constructs of thought and forces of control dominating the dense vibration of our existence.

In looking at thought forms as creators, not only of our own personal reality, but of this beloved world we have come to call home, how does one begin to distinguish between the identity they have attached those thought forms to, and the infinite Self that chose such a critical threshold in which to consciously participate in the shift upon us as a species?

First, you must begin to acknowledge and look at where you are not being authentic within your world. Where, within the many aspects of your reality, is there a discrepancy between who you are as a spiritual being, healer, teacher and powerful creator, and the details you have accepted or resigned yourself to as part of your story?

With compassion and without judgment, every person with any degree of spiritual insight and awareness must become accountable to where attachment and matter have become more treasured than Spirit. We must follow Spirit first.

We have an entire species entrenched in the fear, deception and entitlement of a world veiled in separation. The only possibility for our transformation and evolution as a whole, is in the awakening and emergence of those who agreed to build the new frequency grids and light the way? Does the idea that you are one of a few within the many inspire you or scare you? The answer to that question will reveal how much you are yet attached to form or how much you have been liberated by the intentional work upon your path.

In the past, we have very much taken our expansion process in baby steps, awakening to new realizations and opening to the unknown in increments manageable to the personality aspect. If you take an intelligently reflective look at the state of our planet, our institutions, governments, economy, health and global relations, it is quite evident we no longer have that luxury.

The good news is, because we are now being so supported energetically by the Earth's expansion and the vibrations of the higher realms, we have access to the vibrational momentum necessary to support our leap. The not so good news is, the ego and its attachment to form cannot go with you into the formless unknown. This is just not possible. So, initially, the leap will appear to be your worst nightmare and call to surface wherever your attachments lie. These are the dark forces, shadow aspects and oppositional energy within you that are holding you in limited expression of who you are; enslaved by fear.

Wherever you are in your expansion today, you must have necessarily accreted enough light in the re-membrance of your spiritual identity to understand, in your deepest knowing, that no harm can ultimately come to you and nothing lasting can be taken from you.

The pressing question then becomes, do you want to know your Self, to realize your divinity and to awaken to your full power as a master and creationary being? If you feel the vibration of a yes, making its way from your heart center to your mind, then your Soul is acknowledging that you are ready. The fear that is present is being generated by thought and completely cocooned in the attachments that you have to your illusory sense of self.

Being What You Know

"Now here is one important fact regarding Spaceship Earth
and that is that no instruction book came with it."
Buckminster Fuller

How do we get from where we are today to the vista of a New Earth, when our everyday lives are so compressed with the roles of our identity? How can the Universal Grid, limitless in expression and creative power, influence the matrix of our ego bound reality, when so many cling to the constructs of reality as if it were real and sub- stance giving? How do we pry the ego loose from the life we have so invested our identity in enough to allow our Spirit to expand?

As spiritual beings, we are a field of pure potentiality, a consciousness of presence and joy in the moment. Yet, even the veteran light-workers who have developed spiritual tools and have taught spiritual principles for decades are very much imprisoned by the mind and the attachments it has formed. Their daily practices, choices and nature of relationships may have worked well within the context of a Spirit guided life up until this point, but I am observing increasingly so that many light-workers are feeling less sure of themselves and more fearful of their own limitations.

This is because the intensification of the energies on the planet at this time are such that, all of humanity must necessarily step up in consciousness to flow with the lightwave of the new frequencies. Even those on the path of light for many years must bring a new level of awareness to their 3D constructs and reality. They are no longer out in front of social consciousness so to speak because the new background harmonic of light frequencies are vibrating so finely, many are unconsciously clinging to what is known and provides a sense of safe.

On a daily basis, I am interacting with and observing those who have been intentionally on the path of light for many years, yet are medicating for anxiety and depression, who's physical body is vibrating with density and dis-ease or who are in very dysfunctional relationships and talking themselves around the necessity of looking at the shift that must take place. Practicing spirituality, as a secondary focus to living authentically in your divine essence, is something we are just not going to be able to abide in, and continue to expand. Moreover, how can we possibly imagine the entrenched mindsets and ego bound identities of social conditioning to begin to wake up and be conscious, when we have powerful light-workers who, in many ways, fear the very same unknown?

Recently, a beautiful teacher of the light for over forty years said to me, "how do I know that staying with my husband is not the way to my evolution?" I reflected to her that she had been married for almost 3 decades and that the abusive constructs present in this circumstance were present in two other marriages. Perhaps, (I planted the seed for her contemplation), "perhaps the courage to set you both free from the veils of this illusion is the path to your evolution."

It is so very easy to believe the reasoning of the ego when fear is present. We can come up with inexhaustible excuses to realizing our own power, standing in the center of our truth. You cannot make a decision from your expanded consciousness and a presence of awareness if there is chatter in the mind about the low vibrating constructs of abandonment, victimization, loss and concern for your very survival.

Do you see how insidiously the mind permeates every aspect of our being, so that even when you know the light and have glimpsed the eternal inside of you, you still cling to the illusion of control?

The Universe only knows joy; it vibrates the essence of creative potential, unconditional love, peace and harmony. These are the foundations of the New Earth. You can trust that if any aspect of your life is not resonating with these frequencies effortlessly, then the ego is dictating the circumstances of your reality.

These are definitely not times for the faint of heart or for those who have sensed glimmers of their spiritual power yet are not quite sure they want the responsibility of it. So unprecedented and critical is the time we are in, a time that in your expansiveness, you chose, that we are not going to have the luxury of shifting in a manner that feels comfortable to our illusory sense of self. We are going to have to leap into the nothingness before there is any apparent reality to support us. This is what an evolution in consciousness is about, truly.

Over the course of human history we have advanced greatly in all things connected to the mind, to superior intellect and to the undeniable power of the ego bound identity. Yet, following this course for so long has created a reality of separation, greed, deception and war based solutions to whatever is not complying with the ego's need to be in control; in effect, to be god.

The bringers of the new consciousness are those that have remembered their spiritual identity with enough presence and knowing that they are stepping out of the matrix of form into the formless potential of the unknown. They are no longer looking with a self that is bound by ego concerns, but have moved into a collective, interrelated understanding of this time on planet Earth. They are deliberately and fearlessly surrendering to the unknown, again and again each day, without attachment and are thus, creating the energetic pathways for the many to follow.

This existence is not about us, as egoic individuals, it is about love ~ and creating new worlds of possibility. So conditioned in consciousness have we become to the duality of this dimension, that we have taken it into the essence of our being and have become complacent with the duality within our own lives. Who do you see when you look in the mirror? Who is making the decisions in your reality and can you truly say that you are living an authentic life?

There is an age-old expression about walking the talk, about bringing the consciousness you engage in meditation or connect with in prayer, out into the light of a brand new reality. This is how Christ Consciousness becomes realized; one ungovernable center of beingness at a time, choosing to trust the voice within.

If you are not rising each day full of joy and wonder for the life you live, unceasingly; if you are not vibrating the incandescent light of your authentic radiance while living in harmony, peace and unconditional love, regardless of the structures of form you have built around you, be willing to shift the prism of your own understanding. You absolutely know when you are not vibrating your authenticity. Your responsibility is to your Self as a wise, intelligent super-consciousness. To love all of life and all beings unconditionally is to follow that wisdom above all else and fearlessly leap into the mystery.

Facing Down Fear

"What is sacred? That can only be understood, or happen, when there is complete freedom from fear, from sorrow and when there is this sense of love and compassion with its own intelligence. Then, when the mind is utterly still, that which is sacred will take place.

J. Krishnamurti

It is astounding how much we have come to identify who we are as a species, with form. We are creatures governed by fear. We have given our life force, the expression of our authentic joy, manifestation of our power and the potential of full realization to the mechanisms of this illusion.

It is inestimable how much of whom we are, the choices that we make in our lives and the limits we place upon our being are determined by fear. Fear is the ego's greatest source of sustenance and the antithesis to living in the light, where there is only love and truth. Fear is how the ego keeps us ensnared in the illusion of this dimension and enslaved by deception. It has been said that a person would sell their soul for money and power, which has been demonstrated throughout our history as a species. But those acts of ultimate deception are merely the resulting vibration of fear; fear of not mattering, fear of not being supported, fear of not belonging or being accepted and loved, fear of nothingness and ultimately of death. To the degree that you know fear in your reality, to that extent, you have forgotten who you are and are dependent on a transient understanding of life.

I have had the great gift of having an experiential reality that has exposed me to many walks of life, culture, belief and tradition. This has greatly expanded my own conceptual understanding of how much people internalize their experience throughout life and incorporate those experiences as aspects and reflections of self. In our deepest knowing, we are aware that all circumstances and details of our incarnation were chosen by our expanded beingness to gain emotional understanding and thus, remember that the only Truth, is Love.

Yet, in personalizing the path of our becoming within the conditioning and limitations of the known reality, we have, in effect, been feeding the ego, which thrives on separation and control. You see, the mind, that master computer of our thinking capacity, derives power from separating itself out to find the logic in life. Anything the mind can make sense of automatically engages the ego with the illusion of superiority, of being right and of standing apart from that which doesn't align with the programs already in place. And, of course, the ultimate motivation for anything the ego acts upon or responds to, is fear. Then what? How in the world do we find meaning in a reality created by the egoic aspect of who we are?

All negative emotions evolve out of fear, as well. When we express a negative emotion, in that moment we are experiencing a disconnect from life, from Source, from our Self and ultimately sending that vibration out into the Universal Energy Field to enhance the construct of fear on the planet.

Fear carries the energy of inertia, paralyzing the masses from forward movement and the power to live in their heart.

Fear is the core vibration of the unrealized self and rooted in an extreme attachment to this plane. When you can at least begin to step back from fear enough to acknowledge it as an illusion, you can then enter the process of unraveling its source of initiation, so as to bring light into the deception.

Fear is a manipulation of the mind and a mechanism of dark forces to keep us bound by shadow and untruth. Fear is the dominance of the little mind and limited consciousness over the Universal Mind, of which you are an extension. It is not possible to ultimately know yourself and evolve if you live with fear. We can expand through our fears... so if fear serves any positive purpose, it would be this. But to allow fear to keep you from acting upon or being anything in your expansion process is to give your power away to a deceptive illusion.

One direct and fairly simple way to begin to disentangle your authentic Self from your ego bound identity, is to look at the fears you carry with you in your experience. Imagine who you know yourself to be, the identity you have accumulated over the course of this lifetime, as being a tiny leaf at the top of a most magnificent tree. The leaf, fragile and delicate to the elements, is fastened to a stem, connected to a branch, dependent on a limb, extending from a strong center that reaches effortlessly into the sky. That same pillar of lifeforce reaching into the light also extends deep into the Earth's core, intricately grounded into the eternal sustenance of the Earth's wisdom.

The identity that we assume through the intellect, the mental perception of our awareness, is represented by the leaf, fluttering in the wind. Vulnerable and exposed, there is a lingering sense that our time is limited and that the opportunities within our reach are conditioned by many forces that are beyond our control.

The much greater portion of the tree, with all its multifaceted form and purpose, is the greater Truth of whom you are beyond the illusion of your known; that which makes sense to the egoic mind. It is the strong center that cycles through change with the wisdom of all creation. The unknown portion represents the mystery and is where the ultimate treasures and true power of your beingness lie.

The ego greatly fears the unknown because there is nothing to attach its sense of self and identity to and thus, no place to feed its power. Where there is formlessness, the ego dissolves and the heart's intelligence is allowed to become the informer of experience, purpose and destiny.

Any conscious fears that you carry as aspects of your identity, represent places where you have become fragmented in your beingness. It is as if you had an experience, in this lifetime or one of many, and you left a part of yourself in the form of emotion in that experience. Now that emotion is running a program that empowers the ego. In this way, we are never fully present and ever held prisoner by a past long gone. It stands to reason that if you have conscious fears that restrict your movement, your experience and your freedom in your known reality, then you have unconscious fears influencing your ability to be whole in life, as well. It is a primary objective in mastering the illusion of this dimension to overcome the construct of fear, because fear is the stronghold of attachment and separation. It carries the energy of the temporal over the eternal and gives the very clear message to the ego that loss is a threat it must guard against at all costs. Fear is the single greatest mechanism of control on our planet and the dominant force in the deception that we are finite, limited beings with little to no control over our existence.

In determining to look at everything energetically, which is the only possible way to perceive truth, when you leap into the unknown of your becoming and evolution, your perceptual reality may initially appear worse. This is because we attract to us all of our hidden fears which are no longer veiled by social constructs. We may find ourselves hanging in the dangle of our worst nightmare for a period of time, depending on how much unconscious was present. But, eventually, if we hold center and do not deviate from our intent, we level out, balance, things appear to get better.

Still, because we have moved into the unknown potential and are living by accreting more light versus the nourishment of constructs, as we grow our light, increase our vibration and activate more of our DNA potential, we invite more challenge. Of course, the ego will not like this at all because an increasingly clear portion of its reality is no longer under its power.

As consciousness and a presence of awareness expand, we are moving through and living in more and more rarified spaces energetically. We are here to evolve and grow. Once we wake up enough to accept that Truth, we will be challenged by the density that we pass through as we continue to expand and activate DNA strands of remembrance. The path is a cumulative learning experience. Eventually we must trust that we did not come to this experience for the comfort and ease of the egoic mind, we came here to grow into our magnificence.

So, in your internal reflection and safe perimeter of exploration, if you can simply begin to dialogue with yourself about what scares you in life, a prism of awareness will necessarily begin to shift. Just looking at and acknowledging where you have given power to the mental plane over the heart's intelligence, will begin a necessary unraveling. In your heart's frequency of beingness, which is where your true power lies, you know that you are always safe and that no harm can come to you, because you are eternal.

In that moment when your egoic identity is standing at the edge of the ocean and you fear drowning; when you have a childlike opportunity to ride a double Ferris-wheel and you fear heights; when you remain at a job that offers security but leaves you uninspired, take a moment to be still and acknowledge that those fears are being generated from the power of the egoic mind. The mind then becomes the source of reason for an ego driven existence. There is no judgment involved in this exercise, it is just a decision to not be bound by that which is not real and to create more spaciousness for the unknown truth of who you are to come in and be the new foundation you stand upon.

We are here to engage fully this experience, to master the illusion of our limitations and to fearlessly follow the heart's wisdom in transforming the small frame of reference of the ego into the unlimited expression of the Soul.

"If you bring forth what is within you, what you bring forth will save you. If you do not bring forth what is within you, what you do not bring forth will destroy you."

This quote from the Gnostic teachings has been a haunting voice and guiding force on my path for nearly twenty years. You see, we are here to realize our Self, and that realization comes though the remembrance and manifestation of our gifts. If we live with fear, we cannot fully actualize our gifts because shadows keep them hidden from us. If we walk through life with fears characteristically masking our light and gifts, we are living as only a rudimentary expression of who we are. We are keeping our light beneath the bushel of our fears. In that, you exist as an expression of the constructs of this reality of illusion, and will continue along the course of its fate. If, however, you dare to face the fears of your illusory sense of self, you will be vibrating with the light of your interior essence, and there is no safer, richer, joyful or freer place to be.

"If you go where few have gone, you will find what few have found." Mahatma Buddha

This is another favorite quote of empowerment and validation on my path of expansion. No longer can we abide by the constructs of social conditioning. No longer can we look at what the majority are doing and find solace in the comfort of a known reality. This is a time in the light of all eternity that you chose within which to fulfill the vibrational potential of your ascension. You already are a master in a parallel reality. Go to your future self right now and declare you are ready and willing, unconditionally, to align your personality with your Soul. Remember always that what we want for ourselves, what we desire and yearn for and aspire to as spiritual beings expressing the densest of our vibrational capacity, pales in comparison to what the Source of all the manifested Universes wants for us. We all evolved from the same Light, the same power, the same love, the same infinity. It is who we are and it is an eternal beingness that knows not the illusion of fear.

Turn The Page

"We live in two worlds… the world into which we were born
and the otherworld that was born within us. Both may be a
blessing or a curse. We choose."
Celtic Druid Homely

By now, you are either greatly motivated or in a bit of a funk! I say this with great love and compassion for this often arduous, achingly heart-opening experience that is life. I know well that my job here, as a spiritual being having a very human experience, is to move energy. It is in my core matrix and vibrant energy body to effect change in people's lives within the experiences along my path. This has not been an easy identity for me to integrate into my personality aspect and own fully as my power. It does not lend itself well to developing roots. Often, I need only be present in a person's reality to stir the unconscious aspects of another's interior enough to start a process they are completely unaware of. Because of the light frequency and vibrational intent that came with me into this physical experience, my presence is predestined to shine light into places that need an assemblage point shift (read jump start), to begin a new direction in another's expansion.

My personality aspect would have been very comfortable fitting in, belonging, joining with some person or experience for a lasting known of reality. After 20 years on my path of spiritual awakening, I finally understood all the inter-workings of my 3D reality, my choices and decisions over the course of my lifetime, and was able to see clearly the future unknown. This moment came when my personality lined up with my Soul, as it must for all beings in the process of awakening. I simply knew it was time to turn the page.

Everyone's journey is as unique and varied as we are in frequency and light. If we could but see ourselves in our light frequency, the radiant, glistening field of light spectrum that is our inner essence, our joy would constantly go out before us into experience and create a vibrational opening to glide effortlessly into. Just imagine. One day, very soon, that will be the constant and known of our lives. If you are here NOW, reading these words and integrating this vibrational understanding, you are not only to be a part of the future Earth as an empowered spiritual being, you are ready. So, let us together, prepare you to turn the page.

The way the unconscious thinks about the future is through veils of the past. The unconscious and egoic mind want to know what is going on at all times, so that it can preserve its sense of self. If I were to ask you, on a scale of one to ten, how attached you are to your reality and known identity, what would you say? How important is your routine to you… again, scale of one to ten?

Do you have a certain style that is comfortable and thus important to the way your day flows? Does your hair need to be a certain way to go out the door and the kitchen in a certain order? What happens when the car doesn't start or a person cuts you off in traffic or your credit card is declined while a half dozen people witness the moment?

None of these scenarios is right or wrong, good or bad…. they are just ways for us to observe our emotional nature and the reactive impulse of the ego. They are not who we are and are independent of our constant interior state of joy, peace, harmony, abundance and unconditional love for life and all experience. Awareness is a great illuminator and possesses the vibrational momentum to shift us out of complacency.

In turning the page in your experience from one of maintaining, to an existence of meaningful moments seized for conscious expansion, you must first become an astute observer of self and then be willing to make incremental adjustments to your known. Step out of your comfort zone and do so like you mean it. The more your day flows from routine, the more beholding you are to the influence of the unconscious mind and conditioned self; empowering your false identity to recreate more of the known reality it so craves.

There will be different levels of each person's personal experience from which you can begin to disengage. Many have 3D obligations of set job routines and parental responsibility. Yet, even within the routine, you can bring conscious awareness to not only change it up a bit in flow, but to actively engage the observer, who is ever keenly aware it is all just a story; an illusion. As your consciousness expands and you shift the predictable, you are connecting with the divine mind that sees only a future of unbound potential.

If you are being less than authentic in your reality, if you have a lucid perception of where fear and the little mind have become the primary director of your life experience, STOP. It is time to turn the page and only you can do that. The grace and gift of this NOW on planet Earth is that there is amplified support for this very necessary step to be initiated and acted upon.

There is a war raging on the planet right now and I am not referring to the conflicts the ego engages on this plane of demonstration. The war I speak of is the battle between dark forces and the light. The dark energies are vulnerable and very fearful at this time because as the momentum of this shift accelerates, the frequency of light is growing to assure its victory. The light is always more powerful than darkness and as Gaia continues her cleansing, the mechanisms of control on the planet will resort to dark, dominating and manipulative means to keep people in fear.

Every moment that you engage without a presence of awareness and a frequency of joy and peace, you are opening your energy field to the unconscious influence of social consciousness. This conditioned matrix is an energy of power that is quite deceptive in its cunning to keep you in a state of unaware.

When you defy your own conditioning, you are vibrating with the light frequency of your future and energetically nourishing your light body to show you the unknown way to your actualization and power.

Do not be afraid of who you are. Be vigilant in the awareness of who you are not, and the unrelenting drive of the ego to be the dark master of your known reality.

Sovereignty

"Man is a star - bound to a body."
The Emerald tablets of Thoth, the Atlantean

The spiritual journey can be a very lonely experience. One of the reasons we are so instinctively drawn to be in relationship and to form various reflections of community, is that deep within every being, is the memory of Oneness. What is natural to our essence is a state of union such that there is no sense of separation from anything else.

Then, we are born into a dimension of duality that thrives on separation and the establishment of an identity that has little to do with who we are. As young beings, so innocent and energetically fragile, we are like a sponge that immediately begins to absorb and become conditioned to the understanding and expectations of this reality of illusion.

Of course, this is all part of a divinely orchestrated agreement between who we are as a Soul within the experiences we chose and continue to choose as tools of our becoming. The difficulty arises out of the fact that we don't remember all of this initially, and so set upon a course of learning to conform to what is dictated from without and expected of us as respectable members of the of the human race. Over time, consciousness loses itself in an acquired and false identity, becoming unconscious and ego driven.

For as long as we have inhabited planet Earth, humanity has evolved within the tacit agreement to play by the rules and conditioning of social constructs. We look at what has been and then build upon what has served us well in advancing our intellect and conveniences of comfort… never imagining that we could actually walk in a direction where there have never before been footsteps.

So often we re-create our lives very close to our family origins, be that of a location to put down roots, an education of similar history, dietary choices, professional achievements, religious affiliations and personal lifestyle preferences. This has, of course, changed significantly over the last 40 years, but if you step back and really contemplate how we function as a species, we are very much, conditioned creatures of habit with very little conscious remembrance of ourselves as autonomous, free-thinking, wholly empowered creators.

Relationships are both the curse and the gift of this existence. We energetically attract to our experience those beings that hold a mirror for us of our duality. There is not one experience or relationship from the moment of your physical birth that was not drawn to you by your vibrational signature. Every moment of existence is a beautiful choreography of opposites, magnetized to one another for the purpose of emotional understanding and eventual wholeness. Only that which is the other gives us fully to ourselves.

Yet, relationships also set us up to get lost. We invest so much of our emotional being into the relationships we engage, that the lines of delineation between the two become unclear and distorted. Over the course of a lifetime, we move from one identity base to another, accumulating a greater and greater imprint of association with the false self, so that the ego gains more and more momentum as the director of your destiny.

I remember vividly, as a twenty-four year old grad student, sitting with my Psychological Analysis Professor in his office, after class. He had called me in after previously listening to a recordingof my final. Every student had to answer on audio the question, "Who Am I?"

The most common discourse of response revolved around identities of our known reality. "I am a son, a sister, a mother, an American, an athlete, a student, a Christian and so on.

This Professor of Psychology of nearly 40 years looked curiously at me that day and said that he had never in his career had a student respond, right from the opening statement, the way that I had. I began my reflection with… "I Am a Child of God", and left this erudite man with personal insight into the workings of human nature, speechless.

It is an identity issue for us all, truly. An often excruciatingly beautiful experience of remembering: remembering our light, remembering our truth, remembering our power and the very purposeful reason we chose to be here now.

In order to become whole, to realize our authentic nature and the necessary manifestation of our divine gifts of power, we must begin to move away from the pack mentality of a co-dependent existence. This is much different than living as interdependent organisms, coexisting with life.

As sovereign beings we live and function free of attachments and emotional dysfunction. As a sovereign being, the only fear you have is the fear of not fulfilling your divine destiny, recognizing the other as fellow masters on a journey of discovery. When you begin to contemplate everyone in your known reality as Christ Consciousness that agreed to the role they are playing in your life to assist your mastery, concern over another's well-being and circumstance begins to shift as well, to an awareness that serves to empower everyone.

A great truth about this experience of evolution is, that it is not possible to make a decision for your spiritual identity and highest good, without it being for the highest good of all within your realm of influence.

"But, what about the children," you might ask? "I am a parent with responsibilities to my kids, I can't just suddenly stop being a mom!"

First and foremost you acknowledge that your children too, are spiritual masters, many with more conscious memory of such than adults. And that they chose you to be their parent, as you chose them, for specific gifts of empowerment. They are not to be mini versions of their parent or to fulfill unrealized dreams of some one else's youth. A parent's responsibility is to keep their children safe and be a mirror for the light of their own truth.

If a parent is honoring a child as an individual...is reflecting for him/her the ways of love, compassion, joy and peace in the discovery of their authentic nature, then the parent is fulfilling a contract between sovereign beings. Further, if you are modeling a responsive versus reactive relationship with life, pursuing your dreams, living your heart, loving all beings equally and using your gifts to enrich the lives of others.... then you are being your authenticity and gifting to your children a meaningful and unlimited future.

Beyond the children, it can be very tempting to project your ideals or expectations onto a relationship, making decisions about the other based on what is your need, rather than concern or compassion for another. The arrogance of the ego cannot be underestimated in distorting reality, so that it looks as if you are being more thoughtful or caring about another's well being than your own. Not only is this not honoring the light and mastery of another, it is more often a way to deflect the decisions you are being asked to make and covering your own fear.

Life, existence on planet Earth, the circumstances and conditions that we find ourselves in as a species, is truly unlike any other time in history. This is both heartening and critical in perspective. A transformation is upon us as individuals and as a planet. We can no longer get away with things that could once be swept under the rug or kept in the shadows. The intensification of the light is exposing everything that is not aligned with our highest potential and truth.

Many will make the choice to not remain, to transition off the planet either before or during the profound changes to come, rather than to step up and do the work of their expansion now. And of course, this is a choice and there is no judgment. But to realize the New Earth, an expression of the new consciousness of our authentic nature, we must necessarily lift the frequency of all that we choose to engage, bringing light where there is none.

If we are living love, joy, peace and harmony in all areas of our life of expression, without attachment of emotional distortion, then we will be carried energetically through all the coming Earth changes and dismantling of current power structures.

If we choose to comply, conform and resist where the egoic mind is still clearly in control of our daily reality, we will be swept into the flow of social consciousness and necessarily accept the defeat of the egoic mind and its creations. It is helpful to keep close in conscious awareness that as beings of light, you are always in control with the capacity to change, instantaneously, any aspect of your reality.

Choosing to remain unconscious in any way at a time so marked for victory and transformation is to do a great disservice to your spiritual mastery and the rewards of accepting the responsibility of that sovereignty.

Unraveling The Mystery
Steps on the Path of Becoming

The Tireless Presence of Guidance

"I go forth alone, and stand as ten thousand."

Maya Angelou

I'd like to begin this section with two recent experiences that greatly reflect the constant stream of guidance that surrounds us. First, a dream I had last night.

I was driving on a lone road – isolated, clearly a passage way from one populated area to another. The road seemed to cut through a train warehouse district. I passed a group of people that were sitting outside in a circle. I glanced briefly and could tell that one in the group was some type of law official and the others were listening to him attentively. As I drove, my dog Samadhi Blue in the back as usual... I came upon a slight incline in the road that would peak at a railroad crossing. I could not see what was on the other side of the ascent. Just as I got to the top, a vagrant on a bicycle was suddenly right in from of me, traveling in the wrong direction, and in the middle of the road! We came together, head on.

Leaving the car running, I jumped out of the car after putting on the emergency brake and ran to the man. He appeared fine but I was quite shaken up. Another guy came out of nowhere, literally, and I was apologizing profusely, saying, "I didn't see him", though clearly I was not responsible or at fault.

I remembered the group I had just driven by and said I would go get help. I ran back several hundred yards and went directly to the one that I thought looked like an officer and said, "I just hit someone on a bike!" He immediately jumped up and followed me back to the scene. As we ran, I was replaying for him the whole event. We got to a certain vantage point and I thought I didn't see my car, but dismissed that and kept running. Then we got close enough for me to see that my car was clearly not there…. nor the bike or the two men. Panic set in as I incredulously turned to the officer and said, "it was right there, my car is gone!" Then the greater concern hit me that my dog was in the back seat! He called backup and said not to worry. HA! He would put out an immediate A.P.B. and they would not get far. The cop, of course, was the epitome of calm, cool and collected. Miss Lightworker and evolving being was definitely in reactive mode and caught up in the emotion of the experience.

Back-up arrived and I was telling everything to a lady cop when I had a moment of reflection. "You know those commercials about insurance scams where there are actually two accomplices that set you up," I asked? "Do you think that the two men actually knew each other and set this whole thing up?" She gave me a look that said it happens all the time. And then I started to cry and I said, "I just do not know how to think that way – my mind does not register deception, and they have my dog!!!!!

Well, then I woke up in the middle of the night. The thought of my dog still in the car after it was stolen was the scene that hung on. My mind proceeded to attach itself to a worse case scenario – even though I was awake and it was a dream! There was no way that Blue would have let those men in the car. Period. So - that could only mean they had done something of harm to her! It took awhile for me to let all the imagery go and get back to sleep.

I have been working with dreams both professionally and personally for years. One aspect to my work has been to help people find the deeper meaning that their guidance is endeavoring to share with them through the unconscious state. When something is hidden from our conscious awareness that we are, in fact, ready or needing to shift, it makes sense that it would begin its eventual release in an unconscious state. The greatest thing to remember is that as upsetting or "frightening" as a dream may be to our perceptual awareness.... they are always love, guiding us to a more authentic and conscious awareness of ourselves and the way we are living our daily reality. Without going through the specific details of "decoding" a dream, I worked with key words and imagery in this dream and will share with you the true message.

Dream Message: At this point in my journey and what I am now working on in the conscious awareness of my purpose, I have been moving through the energetics of very set patterns within the central location of social consciousness, the status quo acceptance of what is. Life, reality in the collective unconscious is functioning the way it always has, in conformity. Just before I get to a crossing place, a place to move out of old collective habits, where I can break free of timeworn limitations of social conditioning and take a new, different path or course of action on behalf of the many, I am met head on with the male energy of society; that of dominance, deception and ego. This energy is intent on meeting my energy (representing strongly feminine influence and instinctual knowing) head on and thwarting any more forward movement. The potential was manipulative in nature and intent on stopping the energy of innocence, joy and trust of life.

My guidance was right there, close by as always, and unconcerned. The shadow force was so determined to stop me from crossing over (very relevant to my NOW) that it took away the means. Yet, I was still there, still me, safe, and ready to move forward surrounded by higher forces of light – as we always are. The point of this message from my expanded consciousness is to continue to shift the mental plane when the ego registers fear. We must detach from what is apparent to the eye and keep the focus on the fact that guidance is always there to support us when we need it and to stay in touch with what is true and lasting. Whatever we are personally working to bring light to is always for the ultimate release and freedom of the Collective Consciousness.

Along the same lines of seeing the signposts of the greater meaning of all experience, yesterday I noticed several dead squirrels on the road. "Hugh, you might ask?" Well, where I live, a highly natural and beautiful niche of the world, one very rarely sees a dead squirrel in the road. So, having seen three in one errand definitely had me contemplating. So much so, I am sad to say that I created the experience of actually hitting one myself! In over 25 years of driving, I have never hit a squirrel, yet such is the increasingly creative power of the conscious thinking mind!

I woke up this morning and again, saw at least three or four squirrels squashed on the road as I drove to town. Now, I KNEW something was up energetically. I wanted to determine if this message was personal or one reflecting social consciousness…. so, later that day, when I met a group of students on the trail from our local collage, I took advantage of the synchronicity. These young people are very close to the Earth and attend a school that just happens to operate on the theme of service and a cooperative relationship with nature. I asked them if they had noticed an unusual amount of dead squirrels lately. They immediately concurred that they had noticed more around campus than usual. I then reflected that squirrels are really smart with the kamikaze tactics and that even when you think for sure you will hit one, they always escape! Surely there must be a greater meaning to this unusual event. I shared that squirrels represent busy-ness, activity, and preparedness. Perhaps the message is to STOP the doing and busyness in preparing for an unknown, to be still and go inward and let Spirit guide us to a new way. I definitely had their attention!

The message that I most want convey to you is that truth, clarity, understanding and a clear path of purpose is always available to us. But, you must pay attention and you must do the work of unraveling the clues. There is not one moment of your reality that is not impregnated by unseen forces and clear guidance for your unfolding path of remembrance. We were not given instruction manuals for the ways and reasoning of this plane of existence, humanity has just kind of made it up as it went along. The error and eventual defeat of that plan is that the "rules" of this dimension were created by the ego and the experiences of the pain body.

The guidebook for higher dimensional living and the safe passage to the unknown future on planet Earth can only be found within. To know your self is to know the future, because as conscious creators, we are the greatest reflections of what lies ahead. Life itself is one of the most powerful teachers when the student awakens and is truly ready to learn. There is a conscious intelligence, a living force that is life, and it is in constant communication with you. There are no negative experiences or bad dreams, only the ongoing opportunity to rise up in conscious awareness with a willingness to let the heart's wisdom empower the emotional distortion of our reality. It is all love. We are literally marinated in a love that is the peace, compassion, understanding, joy and forgiveness of our authentic being, times infinity. Be open to the absolute truth that we are never alone, that we are loved beyond measure and that Presence is ever with us to shine the light on the path of our highest good.

Preparing The Vessel

We are cups, constantly and quietly being filled. The trick is,knowing how to tip ourselves over and let the good stuff out.

Ray Bradbury

We are autonomous beings. Like the stars in the sky, snowflakes in winter, the leaves on a tree and the pebbles at the river's edge, every expression of life on the planet is unique. How can that not fill you with the wonder of your magnificence?

Consequently, as spiritual beings, we must find our own way. There is a basic foundation to the evolutionary process that can serve as a springboard for your journey, but it is just not possible for any two beings to experience life from the same awareness and understanding. In each moment, you bring all of who you are and all of your experience to the table, and that greatly informs how you will perceive your current reality. That is why it is so critical to accept that you did not ultimately come here to merge with the energy of others so much as to define your unique gifts of beingness, and then to step fearlessly into that necessary power and purpose.

All the relationships and experiences that we attract along our journey of expansion, are to gain emotional understanding in an area that was previously not whole prior to the experience. From your birth family and location of your birth, your race, personality and body type, to educational choices, marriages and various social identities… all were chosen from your expanded consciousness to assimilate and integrate new levels of vibrational mastery. Once you begin to personalize and form emotional attachments, the ego takes over and begins to manipulate the truth of the current reality with distortions and neediness of the past.

Why is it that we have such vivid memory of the past, yet no apparent memory of the future? We are, after all, living in parallel realities simultaneously and our brains are hard wired to access our future self and time yet to come in any given moment. It is because the ego thrives on the past and a known reality where it can continue to be in control and constantly re-creating from illusion.

Depending on how long you have been on the planet and how much conscious awareness you bring to your reality, there can be quite an intense period of unraveling the attachments to the false identities that the ego has been nourished by over time. The greatest momentum that you can generate in accessing the direct knowledge and information of the Divine Mind, is to begin observing your entire reality and self as vibrational energy, a continuously undulating structure of light. Only then can you begin gathering wisdom and making decisions from an expanded awareness and without emotional attachment.

When you observe everything as energy, it becomes clear where you are gaining power and where you are giving it away. Just become aware that the more identified you are with form, the stronger the ego. Step back from your 3D identity and begin asking why you created an experience and where in it your mastery lies.

As the egoic mind's endless preoccupation with the past and future is brought to the light of consciousness, you are able to depersonalize reality enough to see not your husband, your employer or your mother, for example, but two masters coming together energetically to grow in evolutionary potential. Bringing a presence of awareness to the understanding will bring much illumination to your habits, perceptions, relationships, patterns and choices in how to flow your reality.

Once this step is processed, meaning it clicks in your interior and feels good, even exciting to your conscious awareness, then comes the vigilant mindfulness of looking at each aspect of your life through the discipline of identifying where you are functioning as an emotional expression of the ego and where you are living as a vibrationally empowered spiritual being. Again, think frequency and vibration, consciousness and energy.

As an energetic being, it is necessary to adjust your diet, gradually and over time, to ingest high frequency food: life force: true sustenance for light beings. You are what you eat suddenly takes on a whole new understanding. By eating lifeless or processed foods and primarily cooked foods, you are deadening your internal life force, only nourishing habits of uncreative thought. The challenge, of course, is for you to open your heart and love yourself enough to value and take care of the body temple. The immune system will continue to be challenged. Any unconscious behaviors and negative thoughts and feelings about self will need to be released to continue the expansion process and journey home.

Equally so, how you choose to spend your time represents vibrational sustenance or spiritual malnutrition. Every place you go, begin to ask yourself, is this experience high in frequency or an energetic vampire? An energy vampire is any person or experience that feeds off pranic energy. There is a collective unconscious that lingers anywhere that unconscious thought was present and acted upon. It is increasingly important as you open up to the present moment and determine to know yourself as formlessness, to make conscious choices about the experiences and relationships you engage.

Being impeccable to your own process requires that all interaction with people and experience be of the highest order. Even if and perhaps especially so, you are practicing spiritual principles and bringing more awareness to your private reality, it is wise to guard against the energies of collective dysfunction that are truly a disease on the planet. The more rarified and refined your own energy field becomes, the more important it will be to be selectively scrutinizing in where and with whom you spend you time.

You are constantly engaging frequency and whether you have an awareness of it or not, your whole bio-energetic structure is changing. A partnership of participation requires your willingness to change those neural pathways in the mind that have become habitual versus conscious in awareness. You must begin to relinquish the automatic and unconscious preservation of the unobserved mind to allow the empowered remembrance of your authentic being.

The new energies pouring into our world now through various vortexes are here to assist us and will necessitate that we become more discerning and sensitive to whatever is detrimental to the body. These higher frequency light vibrations streaming in with increasing intensity, the cosmic rays, electrical and magnetic, are recalibrating your receptors to become ever lighter in every sense of the word. We are undergoing an educational process to enable us to live simply and eventually derive sustenance from etheric substance. As you make conscious, positive choices to lift the resonance of your body and your functional reality, you are preparing the vessel of your future self. This is a powerful act of self-love and a statement to the vibratory field that you are stepping up and into your unknown potential.

Living life as a fully conscious, evolving being is to see everything as you. Seeing is freeing. Saying YES to Life, regardless of the conditions of form, is to shift to an uncompromising surrender to what is. Nonresistance is the doorway to a new consciousness, a new Earth and the utter joy of being. There is a joy not of this dimension that is your true nature and is consciousness itself. Joy is not something that comes to you or that you can create from outside of Self. Only by relinquishing resistance and living free from the egoic mind can you live fully in the present moment.

To live in surrender is to defy the ego and all of its distortions, thus developing a tremendously vast, clear seeing, empowered and unconditional relationship with life. This is your key to unlimited possibility, potential of creation and authentic expression of your light.

To prepare the vessels of your physical vehicle through making conscious dietary, social and relationship choices, is to honor all life. In so doing, you are being the mind of God, the Heart of God and the Intent of a New Consciousness that is ushering in a new age of love, peace and harmony.

Traveling Light

"You have to be your own teacher and your own disciple.
You have to question everything that man has accepted as
valuable and necessary."
J.Krishnamurti Freedom From the Known

Close your eyes for a moment and see your body as frequency; light emanating as radiant, dancing energy. As you practice this, play around with the full spectrum of color comprising an expression of your mental, physical, emotional and spiritual essence of being. See the energy centers in your body known as charkas, reflecting your current state of vibrational attunement. As you continue to focus inward, mindful of your vibrational beingness, begin to dissolve the delineation of your physical body and expand your vibrational awareness to include your etheric bodies, and finally to merge with all that is. That is the truth of your being; an infinite, vibrant omnipotent representative of all that has been and all that will be.

Now, come back to a conscious awareness and begin to open your linear capacity of thought to the understanding that, as consciousness and energy, we are responsible creators, living on a vibrational continuum with an in the moment accessibility to the higher realms of existence. With an inherent capacity to know how to live, expand your consciousness and make daily choices based on the wisdom of our intuitive guidance, it is clear that we must move to habits, attitudes and actions that honor our spirituality over our ego based identity. By consciously engaging your power with a nutritional, relational and social understanding of yourself as an energetic being, it is easy to observe how our choices are either feeding the physical capacity of our being with density or creating a new spaciousness within with which to accrete more light and connect in greater depth with our multidimensionality.

Each choice that you make to replace dense, lifeless sustenance with high vibrating life force, you are creating the energetic space to bring in more light-encoded frequency.

Drinking sufficient amounts of water is equally important in clearing out toxins, allowing the flow of current moving through your body to carry information to the intelligence of your cells and central nervous system, which keeps informed of what it needs to stay vital and healthy. There is no reason for the physical body to become diseased if we are putting into it only high vibrational sustenance and lots of pure water.

Equally important to the upkeep and detoxification of the physical body and lymphatic system is exercise. Exercise strengthens the immune system and helps bring your thoughts and emotions into harmony with a higher order of being. Find something that you enjoy so that your ego doesn't create endless reasons to not include a regular routine of movement in your daily life. Engage a mate, child or friend in the goal of daily movement for the body and reap the rewards of not only keeping your own body and mind healthy, but those you care about as well.

It is important to bring your choices and beliefs about life, relationship, self-awareness and personal care into harmony with your future self and primary purpose. Each moment that you keep your energy sovereign, engaging only experiences and persons aligned with your authentic and highest vibration, you are disengaging the unconscious patterns and power of the ego to fill your capacity of potential with more density and emotional attachment. As you continue to replace the inert vibration of matter with the pure intelligent frequency of light within your day to day reality, you are activating the unlimited potential of your DNA codex; your direct link to all the secrets and unknown mysteries of the Omniverse. Guidance becomes effortless, succinct and clear as you consciously engage the indomitable perception of the Divine through your increasingly elevated core frequency.

It is best and more conducive to change to be compassionate and gentle, yet aware, in the process you are engaging. As you continue to "lighten up" your experiential reality, the Divine Mind and internal spaciousness of your being will grow and begin making intelligent decisions for you. Once you reach a certain vibrational capacity, there will be no sense of effort, depravation or separation in your daily reach for authentic power, because your new vibration of conscious awareness will expand to encompass the ultimate union of ALL opposites. You will begin to be what you know.

Creating Sacred Space

"No thought, no action, no movement, total stillness: only thus can one manifest the true nature and law of things from within and unconsciously, and at last become one with heaven and earth."

Lao Tzu

In stillness lies the sweetness of being. In stillness you will discover a contentment, awareness and aliveness that is the I AM Presence; the untouched you beyond this dimension. Stillness is the home of the voice of God within and the understanding of the path that is your destiny. True freedom and enlightenment can be found in the qualities of non-resistance, non-judgment and non-attachment. The quietude and spaciousness created by stillness allows you to detach from the world without, so as to be alone with your Self, developing a relationship of confidence with your magnificence. Stillness gives you direct access to the spiritual dimension where the true meaning of life is revealed and the inner parts of your being are at One with the entire Universe.

Our lives are filled with clutter, things to do and undo, to think, to acquire and to be. The majority of beings cannot be alone for indefinite periods of time without feeling lonely or the need for some form of transient stimulus. Even when we do find or plan the time to be with our Self, it is often sustained by the ego's assuredness that it will be for a known, planned upon length of time. Yes, even in our "scheduled" stillness we are making plans about will come next. Creating sacred space is about creating balance with the fast-paced, time oriented, routine structured demands of the material world. Often our attempts at stillness are so covered up by mental noise that distinguishing between the voice of God and the many voices of your egoic mind, becomes blurred by the possibility of not being in control.

Creating sacred space is a powerful statement to the egoic mind that not only are you setting the intent for greater balance in your life, you are providing a sanctuary and personal space to accommodate the desire to know yourself as an empowered and liberated creator. It is essential to the unfolding awareness of your Self and the high degree of alertness that is needed to be still, to create a sacred space for your spiritual essence; the real you. It can be a whole room or a quaint yet isolated area within a room, but it needs to reflect the receptive reverence of holiness. Your sacred space represents the altar of God within your personal reality, the one place that your spiritual essence can always turn to when the world becomes an imbalanced or threatening place.

Sacred space reflects the intent to give the same dedication, consideration, time and importance to your spirituality as you do the material world. Over time and with practice, not only will your sacred space hold the energy of your expanding consciousness so that you can quickly find the elevated awareness that you continually tap into in the higher realms, but your spirit will begin to gather special relics, treasures, keepsakes, gifts from nature and sacred symbolism that carry the energy of your ongoing transformation. When you begin your stillness and quietude surrounded by the reverence of your true essence, you are literally creating a portal to serve as the transmutation of consciousness into something more, where you can peer into another dimension and see other realities without the determined distraction of outside forces.

The creation of sacred space is about a metaphorical doorway through which you can leave the incessant doingness of 3D expectation and demand behind, surrendering unconditionally to the peace of God.

I have a small chime on my altar. After coming to my sacred space in anticipation of the peace and freedom I find there, I first smudge myself with white sage and then ring a small chime three times. This is a personal ritual that just evolved out of the clear intent to separate my personality self, with all of its demands, from the incandescent expression of joy that is my true nature. You too, will find a meaningful ritual that will become more and more essential and non-negotiable to the unending demands of the outer world. In the ritual and sacred space of your light you will find the still-point of non-attachment where all thought is suspended and the song of your Soul becomes the wise director of your path to enlightenment.

One of the most important elements of your sacred time and stillness is the breath. There are many schools of thought about meditation form; sitting, lying down, in total silence, toning, chanting, staring at an object or looking into the nothingness of your inward focus. All of these are neither good nor ineffective. The purpose of meditation is to enhance your electromagnetic energy field, raising your frequency and bringing all of your senses into the present moment so that you can see, smell, taste, touch and hear vividly the silence within your meditative space. The most important element you can bring to your stillness is awareness and intent.

After setting the background for your spiritual essence to let go within, being aware of the breath as much as possible, observing but not attaching to thought as you deepen, is the single most important thing you can do to expand your consciousness and essence of being. Breath has the power of taking you from thought to formlessness along with the ability to feel the aliveness of your body from within. You are never more alive than when you are still. Breath has the power to take you there. Take deep breaths, observing thoughts and releasing them with the out breath. Concentrate the mind's need to be busy on the inward and outward count of your breath and soon you will find your mind in the bliss of just being. Imagine that. What a gift to your becoming stillness and breath can be. Conscious breath is interrupted thought and over time, you will find the seamless rhythm where there is only you, aware of You, and the infinite truth of your being.

Awareness reflects a consciousness of being conscious; you are fully present, all in one place and wholly available for the higher mind of your Oneness to access all the wisdom and Divine power of your transcendent essence of being. It fills me with wonderment to be present with the awareness that I am not sustaining my breath - my breath is sustaining me! It is an intelligence from beyond this dimension and awareness that is ever reminding me that life is so much greater than the reality of my experience and that I am, in fact, breathing with the rhythm and wisdom of the eternal.

The ongoing benefit of becoming one with your breath in the quietude of your sacred space is that your breath will expand in the awareness of itself and carry on that connection and power in your day-to-day reality. You will begin to mindfully and effortlessly engage the breath throughout your experience as a source of renewal, groundedness and Presence. Breathe all of your reality in deeply from the gut with your hand over your heart; loving and acknowledging the wonder that is life; that is you.

Take time today to prepare an altar for your own beloved god within, to honor life, the earth, all the elements and the four directions. Know that in stillness and meditation you are nourishing yourself and the entire planet, allowing energy to flow through you for the benefit of all. Call upon the wisdom of your future Self, trusting that he/she is waiting in the stillness to gift you the secrets of your unknown future.

Gaia's Gift

In the mist of the morning we open
To all the gifts of the day
We open our hearts and take it all in
and give it all back in our way.
And we sing of the beauty around us.
And we sing of the beauty within.
Oh hear the earth tell that all shall be well,
Anam Cara Anam Cara, soul friend.

Old Shaker Song

The energy that has been building inside of me in anticipation of this chapter is beyond description. The relationship and understanding I have come to know and be from nature is the single most transformative and accelerating gift to my journey.

I am sitting by a river as I write, surrounded by the voice of the Earth's exquisite beauty and the manifestation of the Creator's love for us all. In a daily reality that, by choice, has little known or consistency, coming to and being with nature is the one thing that is a necessary constant in my world. It is with gratitude and joy that I share with you a significant and treasured aspect of who I AM. In so doing, I trust that the Mother's power and gift to humanity will speak directly to the wisdom within you as in invitation to know her essence as your own.

I spent the first thirty-three years of my life in Florida. I had the good fortune to grow up on a lake and was a water baby by nature. I lived to be out of doors, climbing trees, riding horses and spending the night with my best friend in the woods near my home. I am grateful and see clearly how relevant that initiation into life was for my spiritual essence.

But it was not until I moved to the mountains, in a part of the world that is magnificently alive with nature that I truly came into my authenticity of being, and a greatly empowered expression of who I AM. It is my knowing that I was called to the mountains I now call home by a vibrational alignment with my future Self. This is a right of passage, so to speak, that comes to all persons intently on their path of expansion, a call from the mystery to align with a vibration of the Earth's essence more conducive to your, as yet, unrealized potential. Often this "move" will come out of the blue to your conscious awareness and make little sense to the expectations and demands of your known reality. But the inner voice of your knowing will be clear and strong and there will be no question from the practical perspective of the egoic mind that will deter your certainty in saying YES to this unknown possibility of new life. The Earth is an evolving consciousness and as your own consciousness expands, she will call you to places where you may deepen your connection to home.

Our connection to the Earth is incomparable. Gaia is our provider and the wisdom keeper of the cycles of change. She is our mirror and ever inviting us to step into the joy of life. In nature, you discover the sounds of awakening, opening your heart to wonder and the eternal.

There is an intricate interdependent unity in design present in nature that is the template for co-existing in a world of peace. In a daily communion with the earth, you will find the simplicity and sublime truth of all life. Thought, form and all illusion seem to effortlessly fall away as nature beckons your participation. What appears to be separate will begin to merge with you and reveal deeper insights into life and your eternal essence. In the expansiveness of the natural world, there are no expectations, just the unconditional opportunity to be present, aware, seeing and acknowledging. There is but One heartbeat of life unceasingly awakening, cycling and renewing. To commune with nature is to allow her eternal wisdom to move through you as a presence of awareness in your life that is profoundly transformative and freeing to that which is eternal in you.

The evolution of my own relationship with nature greatly accelerated my instinctual knowing and intuitive abilities. In determining to go and be with her, immersing myself in the high frequency of her vibrational life force, I learned to effortlessly release the density of matter that my daily reality exposed me to. I was swept up and redeemed again and again and my psychic abilities began to magnify at an unprecedented rate. What can take years of spiritual study and gathering of tools to awaken in ability were effortlessly downloaded into the etheric and physical layers of my being, because there were not the endless veils of illusion that comprise so much of our waking reality.

I began to experience her vibration as my own awareness and understanding, seeing the spiraling light of her higher harmonic that enabled the lifting of my own DNA codex and consciousness into the higher organized intelligence of the torsion waves now impacting our planet. As we joined in frequency, the trees, flowers, animal kingdom, water and vibrational expression of formlessness began to appear to my perceptual awareness as energy encompassing a full expression of light and frequency. I imagine that in nature, the morphogenetic fields of shared consciousness are amplified in stunning detail.

This greatly empowered my inner sight to transition from the view of everything as form, to the perspective of formlessness where we are able to step back from a me-centered reality of separation and limitation and into an awareness beyond self. I was able to increas-ingly experience my own life with an understanding and compassion for the human dilemma that is the daily reality of many.

The crystalline, electromagnetic grid holding the Earth in a cocoon of truth constantly ushers in new harmonics for the ongoing activation of the DNA: the rainbow serpent of light through which we have access to the language of the living cosmos. I have discovered that living close to the earth, mindful of the elements, four directions, the seasons, the sun and moon and stars, and allowing all that incomprehensible wonder to marinate my being, has greatly enhanced my ability to be excellent at what I want to be and do and gift back to this life.

In listening to and being with the stillness of nature, I began to hear the tones of the higher dimensional realms that every Soul on this planet has access to for the purpose of expanding consciousness. My frequency has become so "lightened" in essence that naturally wild animals give no pause to being with my physical presence, merging their vibrational wisdom of beingness with my own. Just being in the pure frequency of nature greatly enhances your attunement with the mind, heart and wisdom of all Creation.

I have had so many profound, nurturing, healing and empowering experiences in nature that I could easily write a book on that subject alone. I am choosing just a few to share with you to illumine the love that awaits your personal communion with the gifts of the Earth.

I recently began having a most magical manifestation of the Creator's love for me, for us, for life. I have shared frequently with you that choosing to step out of the matrix and surrender completely to the unknown of our potential can often be a daunting endeavor. No matter how long you have been walking the path of your unfoldment, or how much mastery you have gained over the illusions of this dimension, there are always greater levels of awareness and more conscious expansion to rise into. The awakening process is ongoing and our evolutionary capacity unlimited.

I had been integrating and assimilating a particularly intense and seemingly endless portal of transformation, my physical capacity fairly tapped out and drained. Each day, as I went into nature I would ask to be elevated above the misconceptions and distortions of my experience and then filled with what is true.

One day, as I leaned upon a magnificent chestnut tree, I looked beside me in a reverie of contemplation and there sat a perfectly shaped heart rock. It felt as if the entire Universe had stopped in that moment and gifted me the validation of my own heart's intent. The vibration of that experience was stunning in essence. My entire being lifted to a whole new frequency of awareness and I could feel the soft, open and receptive trust of my interior return like a leaf on the wind. And then the joy kicked in so that whatever was heavy laden and veiled in that moment was easily released and replaced with spaciousness

This was the first of what turned into months of being gifted heart rocks. Finding these treasures from the Earth and beyond began to mirror my ongoing experience with undeniable relevance. In my process at the time, I would go into the woods in the throws of the human dilemma, grappling with a newly unveiled challenge, emerging with more hearts, which I had come to understand as a tangible expression of the Creator's love for me, as well as my love for the Creator, and life. Not only were the energies dancing with my current reach, as they always are, they were gifting me something to hold, touch, feel and trust as I moved to a new level of my own capacity.

At first I began giving them away. Every size, color and kind of rock imaginable, they were so amazing that I would intuitively share them with whomever I was guided might need the vibration in some way. I started taking them to my lectures or having one in my pocket to gift to a stranger along my way. I always included the fact that the Universe told me to share this treasure of nature with them so it obviously had energy that was personal to their experience and being. I stopped counting the hearts at the two hundred mark, but they continue to come to me and are placed with gratitude both inside and outside my home. Such is the wonder, the wisdom, the tireless support and love of life for us all.

Do not let the environment or circumstances of your current reality keep this gift from your own expansion process. Even if your only access to the Earth is a city park, go there, with deliberation and openness, asking the mysteries to be revealed. Walking, in any kind of nature is an especially powerful tool of transformation. Walking meditation can be quite effective in releasing the density of the mental plane. Moving the energy of your physical being engages the vibrational fields of your energy bodies. As you fill your thoughts with the pure essence and frequency of nature, the movement of your physical body is literally grounding the higher frequencies down into conscious awareness. I delight in trail running because as my mind is occupied with the focus of uneven terrain, my Spirit is free to soar and gather wisdom. Moving meditation in nature is the greatest therapy on the planet, and it's free!

Finally, no matter whom you are or where you live, you are very much aware of the weather anomalies and the manifestation of environmental extremes such that we have not witnessed or experienced on the planet. The Earth is doing what she has always done, holding up a mirror to reflect not only our misuse of her resources and the consequences of our actions…. she is allowing the cleansing that is necessary for renewal and rebirth. The intensity of unprecedented storms, raging and out of control fires, alarming climate changes, unpredictable shifts in the seasons and even disappearance of some interdependent relationships with the animal kingdom, are all expressions of the gravity of the human experience at this time.

All of our fragmented thoughts, emotions, relationships and unfulfilled yet authentic desires have accumulated in the Collective Unconscious of humanity and the Earth is bearing the angst of that separation and illusion. If you are still and go into the energy of a storm, you will find there the shadow and deception of a species that has lost their way.

When I go to be with the Earth, I feel like I am going home. When friends come to visit and I take them along for the experience, I feel as if I am bringing them to meet my family. I never feel safer, more beautiful, more highly regarded, at peace or loved than when I am in the pristine environment of the natural world.

She has been with us since the beginning of time and will be here long after we are gone. Her constancy and promise of life is a gift of love beyond measure. Take time to go and be with her, listen to the wisdom of her stillness and trust, and she will guide you safely to the future of your highest potential and brightest light.

The Deepening

"You must take a plunge into the water,
not knowing how to swim."
J. Krishnamurti

Walking the path of light is bittersweet. It is the Soul's desire to be here, to live this experience and to move energy through the chaos of separation and duality. The Soul is fearless and once it takes flight in the re-ordering of your known reality, awakening has begun and the ego becomes terrified. It knows that something wise and greater is on to its game. This something greater is consciousness itself.

As consciousness emerges the ego experiences little deaths that can be excruciating to the degree that there is unconscious identification with form. That is the bittersweet nature of the human dilemma and the place where free will becomes magnified in understanding. You cannot run from your destiny, eventually it will catch up with you and engage the reconciliation of the outer with the inner. How you respond to this process is up to you and the determination of your interior to be the future now. No one person will experience life and this rarified opportunity to be responsible and unflinchingly present creators in the same way. Without you, life and the expression of this existence is altered. The dynamic aspect of being that is joy is lessened in the world without your conscious participation. "Why go to all this trouble, "the mind may ask?

In a word, love.

The hour of the Soul is the entrance of grace into a very limited experience; a Presence that allows for a shift from doing to being, of running away from to emerging into an inconceivable nothingness where we can break free at last from lifetimes of unconscious programming and illusion. To expand and evolve, which is an inevitable and irreversible process once begun, is to view life and all experience from the level of the Soul. The Soul is here in search of real life, to find its voice within the contraction and limitation of this dimension, even as the ego determines to conform and recreate the past out of fear. To find meaning in existence, the genetics and history of all you have known and been must give way to the Soul's urging and an ongoing dissolution of the egoic mind. The Soul carries the memory and discerning voice of your Spirit, the awakening of the warrior within.

Everything that is life is consciousness (God) and energy; the many levels of vibration and frequency that exist in relation to form and formlessness. It is a process of unspeakable grace that every Soul engages to expand into new levels of Mastery as a Spiritual, Ascended Being with an ever higher purpose and calling then previously realized.

The duality that is this dimension reflects that life is two fold in nature, comprising an inner and outer expression of beingness and purpose. Initially, we are thrust into the density of matter and life becomes a lesson in survival. Once we reach a certain level of awareness and remembrance, we begin consciously choosing that which nurtures and grows our light frequency, so that we can rise above mere survival and the contraction of the mental plane, creating space for meaning and purpose to come in; the aligning of the personality aspect with the Soul's intent. Each choice, decision and step forward in conscious awareness to engage higher frequency, accelerates where you are in that moment and increases your vibrational momentum to be present and One with Universal Intelligence.

As the observer (your higher aspect) awakens and becomes empowered within your everyday reality, you will be able to separate who you are from your thoughts and develop discernment in distinguishing your authentic voice from the voices of unconscious programming. As you accrete more light, you will know what to do for your own process and empowerment. Once you have surrendered the identity of the outer being to the inner being of your wisdom and true nature, the expansion process, different for each, can truly begin.

At the beginning of my spiritual awakening, I was walking the path of light with awareness and applying spiritual principles while still very much supported by and intertwined with my physical identity. After nearly twelve years in a profession chosen by the conditioning and understanding of my youth, I was prompted by what can only be grace, to leap into the unknown of the mystery.

I call it grace because your process, your expansion, your evolution, cannot be forced. It can be allowed, nurtured and accelerated by the presence of awareness and conscious choices you engage, but the journey of spiritual awakening is about attuning your vibrational capacity with the frequency of Source energy. It is an inside job and certainly not another achievement for the ego to attain that necessarily creates more bravado of self-importance. Evolution is not a concept, it is an awakening. You must clear what is inauthentic, false in desire and vibrationally dense so that your true essence can begin to re-order your unconscious and egoic creations.

I was highly regarded and successful within my chosen profession, very content with my life. I loved what I was doing and there was value in its contribution to conditioned society. Yet, I was aware that there was compartmentalization within my known world - I was playing many different roles and feeling the inner pull of a spiritual urge that needed to expand. I intuitively knew and began to connect with an awareness that gave me a view of future potentials. I saw clearly how my current reality was not fully supporting the greater transformation of my own path and the future Earth.

Through an intricate and truly mystical succession of inner promptings and outer experience, I could feel a whole other world unto itself emerging to a more conscious presence and influence over my everyday flow of life. As I allowed, accepted and gave more intent to that flow of divine inspiration, following through on the simplest, to potentially life altering of intuitive impulses, I was given more guidance and clear steps into an exciting, albeit frightening unknown. The more I said yes to the interior of my knowing and formless wisdom, the more my ego would squirm and my mind busy itself with mindless chatter.

As I began stepping back from my egoic restlessness and dropping into an emerging essence that responded to my anxiety with more inspired thought and creative possibility, I was given graceful mirrors within my routine that allowed my physical energy to begin to grow in equal proportion to the conscious work that I was doing and engaging within the higher realms. Enthusiasm grew as I created the space for more nothingness to enter, accepting that as my consciousness expanded from within, my ego that enhanced itself from without would become extremely uncomfortable.

Within a year of this prism shift in my awareness and greater understanding that for new to come in, old must dissolve, I found a necessary surrender between the need to be in control and know, and the complete joy and expansiveness of the mystery of life. The world is just so vast. I began to contemplate deeply how very little of it we see in comparison, within the well-ordered maintenance of a known sphere of influence, which seems to become more and more complex in conditioning as we grow and "settle" in to what is. Each moment, we have a choice to contract and stay within the safety of what we know and the comfortable identification the ego enhances itself with in familiar surroundings. Or, we can choose to expand, trusting a voice and intelligence outside our limited perspective of experience to illumine a new path.

I began to seek a new counsel within that increasingly guided me in conscious action to balance doing with being. Curiously, without knowing what it was, friends and colleagues started noticing a new glow, a radiance emerging that I would come to understand as the light of my inner being, hungry for spaciousness and room to grow, shining through from the former veils of conditioning I was now releasing in my surrender. I no longer belonged to my self, I was suddenly swept up by my own higher intent to know my Self: the formless, creative, intelligent force of my spiritual essence.

As my ego and attachments dissolved, I found myself resigning and moving across country to an unknown reality with no job or familiar relations. My spirit felt immeasurable freedom in the unlimited potential and wide-open space this decision created, but my ego was in great upheaval. Suddenly, my outer world made little sense because I had removed many of the foundational constructs I had so come to accept as part of my identity. I had to undergo an adjustment period that I called "hanging in the dangle", where there is no sure footing and varying degrees of chaos. I came to understand what Anais Nin meant when she reflected, "life shrinks or expands in proportion to ones courage."

It was a time of assimilating and integrating a new sense of Self. I was standing on the shoreline of a vast ocean where the tide had gone out, ready for a new level of spiritual power relative to my willingness to be uncomfortable, until the rhythm of my new reality began its return flow.

It was easily the best thing that had ever happened in my life until that point. Everything looked and felt different as I began the process of aligning with my primary purpose, trusting my Self and trusting life. I had entered a deeper, unknown of unmanifested potential…. the isness of all existence!

As I continued to accrete more light and relax into trust, my unveiled core vibration began to attract to my reality the persons and experiences of my authentic and radiant Self. Instead of existing in the tightly bound field of my known reality of frequency, synchronicity increased exponentially, empowering me to be in my heart and present with the nothingness.

Once synchronicity attunes to your spaciousness, you will not recognize yourself or the world that you once knew. You will be in a state of wonderment as to whether or not you knew then that your former life was not the real you! It was a time of becoming intimate with my Self. I learned instinctively in this stage of my awakening that there were few if any that I could share my experience with. I dared not invite incredulous expressions and well-meaning but limited perspective on the increasingly out of the box choices I was making with my still, as yet, fragile courage.

When I brought to surface new found fears and doubts, that initially translated into resistances and blocks in my 3D reality, my personality self wanted sympathy from my outer world. Yet, knowing that victim consciousness is all too easily engaged and reinforced, I kept much of my internal process and passing illusions to myself. The ever-expanding path of awakening, of becoming conscious and fully present is challenging enough for the one engaging the choice. To ask another, especially those that are close to you in connection, to get into the shadow of your unraveling with you, is often not so much for compassionate support as for sympathy and egoic indulgence. I determined to go inward and connect with that which is eternal, wise, all seeing and expansive; a new order of being was upon me and my ego was no longer in charge.

A great gift of many in the expansion process is that whatever ground you gain in emotional understanding and freedom from the prison of attachments, is never lost. Once transformed, the light of that density and the current strands of DNA are then lifted to a new and permanent level of being. When different stages of our physical agreements and contracts are complete, we are reborn in other realities as well, sending vibrational impulses of liberation throughout many incarnations and dimensions. The more I let go, surrendered and detached from the passing illusions of my ego's attachments, the more my innate joy was able to emerge without fear of loss and anxiety.

Life began to lift me up above the transience of all form and show me the higher light of my own process. I found myself whistling and humming for no apparent reason, in spite of everyday challenges and the shadows of a dissolving identity. I discovered that I could live my personal truth while honoring the journey of others when I shifted my perspective to acceptance that everyone is walking a path of personal choice. That the same organized and intelligent force that is responsible for creating life, as we know it, is inside of everyone else, as well as me. We are all experiencing extensions of the eternal, making our way back to Self.

Every breath that you take is so very significant to the transformation of your being, as well as the transformation of a species. The possibility of a new Earth is dependent on a new consciousness, one that creates from an awakened, vigilant presence of awareness. The future is now. It is how you are being in each moment. The Soul searches within lifetimes for such epic times as this now for planet Earth. We are poised to move through this cycle of change with an unprecedented transformation in consciousness. Empowered by the Earth's natural rhythm and the support of the most expansive frequencies ever available for the purpose of surrendering the known of our understanding to the unknown of our dormant potentials, we must set our minds upon lofty thoughts and realize that this life and our place within it is much greater than what we have yet dared ourselves to reach for.

The Freedom of Love

I would believe only in a god who could dance. And when I saw my devil, I found him serious, thorough, profound and solemn: it was the spirit of gravity – through him all things fall. Not by wrath does one kill but by laughter. Come let us kill the spirit of gravity. I have learned to walk: ever since, I let myself run. I have learned to fly. Now I am light, now I fly, now I see myself beneath myself, now god dances through me.

Friedrich Nietzsche

Beyond all time and space, within and outside all known and unknown dimensions, a pause between the inhalation and exhalation of prana, there is a void where all realities and planes of existence collapse into themselves: a nothingness of penetrating stillness and silence. It is the womb of all creation. In that nothingness is a superluminal pulse, a heartbeat of dominant desire and primary purpose, the unknown giving birth to a known of many worlds of expression and beingness. This void beyond the exploration, technologies and intelligent scope of the most superior life force, initiated life as we know it and beyond, out of supreme love and the desire to experience the totality of Itself; to manifest unlimited consciousness.

We are the experiencing extensions of the Eternal, the void out of which the entire cosmos evolved: every galaxy, every planet, every star, every atom and molecule, all species and intelligence. Our path in life upon this plane of existence is to realize the god within, to dance with the duality of separation and go beyond the limitations and illusions of this dimension. It is in embracing all life, its pain and its shadow, its wonder and its bliss, its distortion and brokenness, beauty and sorrow, joy and divine union that we gather up the lost pieces of a forgotten god. In truth, we are One with the unknown God of the great beyond.

The essence of who we are, all that we have been and all that we will be walks side by side with a benevolent, loving, all powerful Presence that is God Consciousness; we are in partnership with magnificence.

There is a golden plane of bliss that knows our eternal nature as its own, delights in our being and imbues our internal spark with the teachings of the Inner Christ.. In the crystalline expression of our multidimensionality, we know only love, a desire to contribute and the remembrance of these powerful teachings. There to guide us in how to deal with unseen, low vibrating influences, how to manifest with a wise, discerning, all knowing intelligence and how to maintain the energies of our inherent light, these emanations of our pure and vital nature assure that we are ever receiving guidance of the highest level.

In this remembrance, we have the infinite capacity as Light surrounded by Light, to communicate with consciousness itself; a vibrating realm of thought to thought transmission with holiness. The only thing asked of us in this chosen involution of beingnessis to go forth with openness of mind, loving hearts and pure intent, into the lessons of our becoming. The treasure is in knowing that love is the greatest power and the light of all eternity, present in each moment, through our acceptance and allowing of what is.

Love summons the Source of all Creation to heal; to realize that all persons and experiences are our thoughts made manifest, that they reflect what we expect to see and that expectation is a powerful creator of our reality; positive and negative. Every experience is an opportunity to love and forgive where we have forgotten whom and what we are. To perceive the innocence and Christ Light in all expressions of life is a choice to evolve back into a state of Unity. Just to be here in this experience, having so much abundance of life and beauty unceasingly available to us is a gift beyond measure. Everything else is detail.

There is not one moment that Christ love is not illuminating the path to our divine essence, not one moment that whatever or whomever we are beholding is not there to help realize the Christ within.

We are awakening from a perpetual sleep of forgetfulness, to the evolution of our potential. We have experienced deeply the consequences of creating from the ego's desire to attain power in the known of a very transient existence. Within the current revolution of consciousness destined to be the portal to a new understanding and expression of manifested life, we have the capacity to step back from a very limited perspective of who we are enough to see that any person or experience that we perceive to be less than or other than ourselves, stands between us and our path to God.

I remember teaching Sunday school to the children of my Methodist upbringing: the me I once was. I was never sure, as a young person with a newly emerging sense of individuality, that what I was doing within those four walls with those impressionable beings would be approved of, but I was listening to my heart and trusting in a love that superceded division and separation. I would gather the young and innocent around me and share that there were children in that same moment, in Sunday School over at the Catholic church on the corner, who believed with all their heart that what they believed and practiced was the way to the love of God. When we are all praying to the same God from a conditioned illusion of exclusivity and entitlement, what does God do?

We live in One World. All life is just as sacred and precious to the Creator of it all as any one expression of its potential. We were all once innocent children and when it comes to the awareness and understanding of what the totality of Creation is all about, we are children still. What is it that allows us to rise above our own mediocrity and fear to the remembrance of what the beloved master Jesus taught; that like Him, we are the likeness and image of the One God; endowed with the magnificence and potential of Infinite expression and power.

We can choose to continue to create in fear, separation and judgment, manifesting the division and sorrow of illusion. Or, we can allow the unspeakable grace of our own truth to enter in and set us free from the prison of our unconscious minds.

To know gratitude is to accept the responsibility of who you are; the way, the Truth and the Life; God made manifest into flesh, as is everything that is life in existence. It is all God, it is all me, and it is all you. When you experience life with the compassion and understanding of your heart, you are resonating and seeing with the Mind and Heart of God rather than the conditioning and mindsets of those governed by fear. You can experience and instantly release what is seeking forgiveness in yourself and others who have lost their way. It matters not what a person has done or how they choose to experience life, they are loved and forgiven before they even stray.

There is nothing to fix, only more Self to realize. The practice of acceptance, of unconditional love and forgiveness in each moment, opens the spaciousness within your own confinement to invite gratitude in, transforming you and your experience into one of freedom.

Gratitude is the quality of relinquishing all effort to the greater truth that everything and all life are gifts. Accept whatever and whomever you are without judgment. There are no right or wrongs, only wisdom to be gained. Everyone is doing the best they know how from the experiences and reflections of their known reality. When you have compassion and forgiveness for your own experience instead of focusing on the perceived transgressions of another, you are transmitting a revolutionary teaching, giving others permission to find compassion for themselves, which will then ripple out into their lives and experience.

One of the most profound moments of my life happened when I was standing at the kitchen sink, washing dishes. I was talking to the higher realms, asking for some tangible reflection that I was walking the well-lit path, aligned with the heart and mind of the Creator. And in that moment I had a prism shift that shimmered through out all of who I knew myself to be and as yet dared to reach for. The insight of revelation was that who I Am, my heart of intent and love for life.... is the answer to every prayer I have every prayed. To experience unspeakable grace is to know profoundly, that even the trials and challenges, the heartbreak and mistakes, the less than stellar moments and the complete undoing of who you thought yourself to be… is a gift from the future of your potential with absolute faith in your ability to rise above all illusion. In that moment, you are transformed.

Only those who have experienced the hour the soul truly makes itself known, when the soul starts to speak that it is ready to do the work it was sent here from the light of all eternity to do, can fathom this inexplicable urging from within. No longer searching, the Soul has been given the space for you to now seek your own counsel. Gratitude is no longer a quality to extol, it becomes the very heart and essence of your presence, endowed with the capacity to find beauty and meaning in just being. Then there is nothing and no one to forgive because it is all just one endless expression of the experiential fullness and beauty that is all life.

"My experience of God is not so much as a deity
but as a profound sense of wonder.
Albert Einstein

It is only with the heart that one sees rightly,
What is essential is invisible to the eye.
Antoine De-Saint-Exupery

Bridge Across Tomorrow

"Someday perhaps the inner light will shine forth from us,
and then we will need no other light.
~Johann Wolfgang von Goethe

The only way to affect change is through conscious action. Start where you are and call forth the dream living within. It is only through heart centered, harmonious and selfless acts of the individual spirit that Universal Spirit and Unity Consciousness can be birthed.

The path of awakening is born of conviction, courage and remembrance. These three pillars of stewardship reside in the authentic nature and heart center of each individual. It is a template of being and living in a new world that was the original vision for this beautiful blue planet; the divine union of the outer with the inner, the higher with the lower, of heaven and Earth, of a God without with the god indwelling.

Any act of meaningful and lasting consequence requires heroic and dedicated self-effort; individuals seemingly separate yet expanding in consciousness to stand side by side with an absolute faith and centered knowingness of the Collective Enlightenment upon us as a species. Within you there is a placeholder and communication medium designed to conspire with the stars for a collective union of the soul, the spiritual and creative essence, with the conscious mind of each individual.

Living an inspired life is being attuned to the totality of life, the God essence and creative empowerment of the heart's intelligence.

When we live primarily from the limited expression of the mind we will always be in a reactive mode of being. The heart's wisdom is a direct link to the mind of God, the unknown, and a responsive trust in Self and Life. In conscious presence and awareness lies the key to our future.

We are vibrationally encoded to be authentic, enlightened members of the greater family of light. Recognizing that we all have the total Truth inside of us in each moment, this time of wonderment and Oneness Awareness becomes a joyous allowing of our inherent and sublime spiritual seeds to begin to germinate. In the germinating, the golden threads of luminous light begin weaving a morphogenetic field of right timing, right understanding, right action and righteous love to unite those of original intent with their heart's awakening.

We all have a common yearning to be of service in the global enlightenment of our species. But more than that, the purpose and role of intent we all agreed to is being activated through the love and profound wisdom of the Earth.

All along, wherever your journey has taken you and whatever experiences you have known, each person's goal was and will always be, love. In that realization, the question always comes back to loving all that is and ever asking how we can unite with one another in a moment, a purpose, a dream and a vision of mutual compassion and cooperative effort.

There is only one message behind whatever your belief or spiritual practice is – we are all One. We come from the same

Source, the same light, the same peace, the same love and will return to that inexplicable origin.

The new human, is indeed, an intent whose time has come. In our brightest light, we aspire to the highest frequency of our capacity as creationary beings of wisdom, beauty and peace. The untapped potential in our individual DNA is acknowledged as a resonantly attuned antenna capable of intergalactic communication with worlds and dimensions beyond the density and fear of this reality; higher dimensional realms of benevolent wisdom and technology that can be shared with humanity at a time when living in peace is no longer a dream but the only possibility for a future Earth.

The time is upon us to live the Universal principles of love, peace and harmony with our brothers and sisters within our own species, and with all intelligent life. For too long, the many on our planet have sought power for powers sake. There are higher levels of consciousness with advanced technologies that want peace; highly evolved civilizations that have been interacting with the Earth throughout its history. In order to communicate with them we must raise our consciousness to where they are, offering the best, positive and spiritually motivated intent of who we are rather than meeting them with fear and warfare.

Reality unfolds as a result of how we are being. In choosing peace, we choose conscious evolution within our own species as well as an intelligent cooperation with a spiritual hierarchy willing to work with us toward an age of Universal Unity.